YOU ARE BECAUSE HE IS

Speaking the life, death and resurrection of Jesus over our children

ANNALISA BARRAZA

Copyright © 2024 Annalisa Barraza.

All rights reserved. No part of this book may be used or reproduced by any means, graphic, electronic, or mechanical, including photocopying, recording, taping or by any information storage retrieval system without the written permission of the author except in the case of brief quotations embodied in critical articles and reviews.

WestBow Press books may be ordered through booksellers or by contacting:

WestBow Press
A Division of Thomas Nelson & Zondervan
1663 Liberty Drive
Bloomington, IN 47403
www.westbowpress.com
844-714-3454

Because of the dynamic nature of the Internet, any web addresses or links contained in this book may have changed since publication and may no longer be valid. The views expressed in this work are solely those of the author and do not necessarily reflect the views of the publisher, and the publisher hereby disclaims any responsibility for them.

Any people depicted in stock imagery provided by Getty Images are models, and such images are being used for illustrative purposes only. Certain stock imagery © Getty Images.

Scripture quotations are taken from the ESV Bible® (The Holy Bible, English Standard Version®), copyright © 2001 by Crossway Bibles, a publishing ministry of Good News Publishers. Used by permission. All rights reserved.

ISBN: 979-8-3850-2976-1 (sc)
ISBN: 979-8-3850-2978-5 (hc)
ISBN: 979-8-3850-2977-8 (e)

Library of Congress Control Number: 2024915117

Print information available on the last page.

WestBow Press rev. date: 09/16/2024

CONTENTS

Introduction vii

Brave 1

Kind 9

Worthy 17

Whole 23

Good 31

Wise 37

Beautiful 45

Wanted 55

Gentle 63

Needed 69

Loved by God 75

Loved by Mom and Dad 83

Unchanging 91

Acknowledgments 97

INTRODUCTION

When I set out to put my thoughts, really my prayers, into words, I had one goal in mind: that our girls would know the faithfulness of our Father. Then I started writing, and the desire to share it with others I have crossed paths with during our many military moves grew deeper. I could have simply shared the manuscript with all of them and then stored it away for my girls to read one day. But I also want them to know that our Father dreams with us. I dreamed of having a book in the world. I dreamed of it every morning as I joined my Father in the secret place. I wrote it down and said, "Lord, if it be your will, bless it." I don't dream alone, and I don't dream to simply hold onto them. So to be the example I long for our girls and for my young nieces to live up to, my only choice was to put it out in the world for you to read too. And if it only ever blesses just you, thanks be to God.

My early teenage years were rough, but I'd say my

late teens and early twenties were rougher. I questioned everything I thought I was because I really had no clue who I was. Mistakes were made, and redemption held out its hand to me from an empty tomb. Somewhere in the middle of the struggle, the Lord gifted me the most precious baby girl. I would reflect on my struggles often during the first year of motherhood, asking the Lord to spare my own daughter the same struggles. It was from that desperation our daily saying came to be.

One night, I looked my infant daughter in the eyes, and I told her everything I wanted her to remember about herself: "You are brave. You are kind. You are good. You are wise. You are beautiful. You are gentle. You are wanted. You are needed. You are worthy. You are whole. You are loved by God. You are loved by Mommy and Daddy. There is nothing you could do that would change these things ever."

In a lot of ways, I was speaking to myself, the young twenty-three-year-old, the young mom who had no idea what she was doing, and the mom who didn't know these things about herself yet and didn't fully know how Jesus made her these things despite herself. I loved the idea of my daughter knowing these things long before she was like me, a mom and still searching. While saying these things to her and pressing into my relationship with Jesus, I would come to own these things as well.

Eight years and three more beautiful daughters later, we still say this to them. Only now, my relationship with the Lord is deeper and growing. These words have a much deeper meaning to me and to them as we learn who our Messiah is and what He has done for us. It's because of Him that they are all these things. It is because of the heart of our Father that I can tell them these things with so much confidence and assurance.

It's because of Jesus that I can confidently share these with you. Within these pages, you will find the why— why we can own these things as young women or as young men. Our daughters will find the why behind all of these. You will find the why behind all of these. Why am I brave? Why am I kind? Why am I loved?

Because if you're anything like me, there will be a point in your life where you will question all of these. Am I brave? Am I kind? Am I loved? You'll look at your mistakes, your circumstances, your environment, and you'll question. If you've been there, if you are there, I pray these words speak right to your heart. This is a love letter from our rescuing Messiah to you.

I've had the great opportunity to speak to groups of women within the ministry, and I will begin this book the same way I begin those teachings, which is with a prayer.

Heavenly Father, may Your Holy Spirit take over these pages. May those reading this see Your hands and work in their own lives. May they remember who You are and what You do for them daily. Thank You for our identity, for calling us by name, and for remembering us in every moment. Thank You for our living and moving

Messiah who sits to intercede for us forevermore. May You bless these words with Your glory, and may You bless those reading this with Your glory. In Jesus's name. Amen.

BRAVE

And David said, "The Lord who delivered me from the paw of the lion and from the paw of the bear will deliver me from the paw of the philistine." And Saul said to David, "Go, and the Lord be with you."

—1 Samuel 17:37

One night after we had gone to eat with some friends, our four-year-old at the time fell and scraped her knee in the parking lot. That's it. That was the end of the world as she knew it. It was our job as her parents to walk her through her personal Armageddon. After making sure her knee was OK, we began to help walk her through the pain and heightened emotions after what just happened.

As I sat there taking deep breaths, trying to show her one of our calming strategies, I remember crying out from my heart, asking the Lord to help me help her. It was after that prayer and between my toddler's blood-curdling screams that I remembered our word of the week and our verse. The light bulb in my head went off as I praised our faithful Father. I immediately turned to her and said, "He delivered me from the paw of the—?"

She took a deep breath in and replied, "Lion."

We continued. "He delivered me from the paw of the—?"

"Bear!"

"He will deliver me from the paw of the—?"

"Philistine!"

I continued to say, "Remember our word for this week? Brave. Even though it hurts and even though you're scared, you're still brave because God is for you. It's who you are because of Jesus."

The tears slowed as she leaned in for snuggles and nodded her head. At that moment, when her world was falling apart and she was sure she was done, she just needed to be reminded that she was brave. Does that feel as close to home to you as it does to me? There are moments in my own adult life when I feel done, too numb to move forward and need someone to remind me that I am, in fact, brave. That is just because we don't feel it at that moment doesn't mean it's not who we are. But, friends, our feelings don't get to dictate our identity. Not ever.

That's it, isn't it? We tend to believe that because

we can't feel our way out of our fear we have to disown our kingdom's bravery. But it's in those moments where we can't muster up the feelings that our identity gets to shine. Where the end of ourselves has come and all that is left is the one who can fill us anew. Our Messiah has full freedom to be the light in us through the Holy Spirit in this place. This place where there is no more of you left. Where there is less of us, there can be more of Him.

We can look at something, feel fear, and yet still be brave because our God is brave for us. Our God holds the bravery that we can't muster on our own. We just have to trust that He is who He says He is. That's a loaded statement, isn't it, dear friends? How do I just trust Him?

For that, we look to the example David gave us. We look at the words our Father left us, and we put them into practice every moment we can.

When face to face with something very real and very scary, David remembered His God. He remembered his days of shepherding when he faced beasts that could have ruined him and the sheep he was in charge of. He then said out loud the moments when he was delivered by the hands of his Father two times before.

In 1 Samuel 17, we see David recall how he went to face a bear and a lion while he was shepherding. He recalls this and states the truth of those situations in order to confront the Philistines in front of the Israelites. He says, "The Lord delivered me from the paw of the lion, He delivered me from the paw of the bear, He will deliver me from the paw of the Philistine."

Now we do know that context matters. David was heading into battle for the people of God. He played a big role in the redemption story that led up to our Messiah, Jesus. We aren't David, and we aren't the Israelites. Oh, but aren't we children of God on this side of the Messiah? Aren't we fighting these battles, both big and small, for the sake of the kingdom?

Every time we call on the name of the Lord to help us

You Are Because He Is | 5

be brave, Jesus brings the kingdom one day, one moment closer. So if we know we too are the children of God with big parts to play in the kingdom, then we must know that we can use the example David laid out for us.

Have you ever been delivered from something through the hands of your Father? Something you've gone to face and the Lord brought you out of?

Think back to a struggle you no longer are experiencing, or a pain that doesn't plague you like it once did. Can you see God's hands in it now that you're on the other side?

Let's take the example of David and be like him. Grab those two things the Lord delivered you from and the one really scary thing that is plaguing you now.

Got them? Now let's be like David.

"He delivered me from the paw of __" (Fill in one of the things the Lord has overcome for you.)

"He delivered me from the paw of __" (Now the second.)

"He will deliver me from ___" (Now fill in something plaguing you now.)

I'll give you mine right now in this moment, which, if you keep reading, you'll get more insight on.

"He delivered me through the pregnancy of our oldest, He delivered me through the pregnancy of two more, and He will deliver me through the pregnancy of another."

We can remember what our Father brought us through and speak that truth in our moments of fear. The truth is that we don't have to live in that struggle or fear anymore because we have been delivered. We can remember how He delivered David, the shepherd, from the paw of the lion, the bear, and the Philistine; made him a king; and brought him to a place that would allow our Messiah to come forth.

We can remember that we are also the children of God called to call on Jesus to bring forth the kingdom to those around us. We can let Him bring us to the place

He has for us in the kingdom. We can let Him help us be brave.

You are brave, dear friends, because the Messiah who died and rose for you is brave.

KIND

But the fruit of the spirit is joy, peace, patience, kindness,

goodness, faithfulness, humility, self-control.

—Galatians 5:22–23

When I was around eight years old, I saw two quarters on a big popcorn tin. They were not mine; they were my brothers'. You know those tins, right? Boy Scouts were selling them every year, and they were full of different flavors of popcorn. Yep, those. And I know fifty cents doesn't seem like a lot, but back then, it could get me a bag of chips out of a vending machine, OK? I digress. The point is he had left them there, and he was nowhere to be found. Temptation came over me. I don't even remember why I wanted them, but I did. I probably wanted the Hot Cheetos from the vending machine at school. Regardless of why, I knew I wanted his two quarters. So I took them. I took what wasn't mine.

Later that evening, my brother was looking for them and brought my mom into the hunt. I hid in my room, waiting until they gave up the fight. A knock on my door came a few moments later, and my mom walked in. She asked me if I took them. There it was, my chance to tell her the truth and to hand over what I had stolen. So you know what I did? Correct. I lied. I said I didn't. She probably gave me a really good speech in a very roundabout way that stealing is wrong and telling the truth is best, then she walked out. Moms always know what you think they don't.

Guilt ate at me. Not only had I been mean and stolen from my brother, but I had also lied to my mom. I sat there in guilt and shame for who knows how long. Finally, I couldn't bear it. In tears, I ran to my mom and told her everything I had done, holding the quarters out for her to take and ready for the punishment for what I had done.

This moment in my childhood obviously had a huge emotional impact on my life. Those of you with some psychology background or passion are probably already analyzing the implications it could have had on me. You'd probably be right in a lot of ways, but it was what happened after I gave the coins back that had the larger impact on my life.

I remember having to hand the coins to my brother myself and apologizing to him. Then I remember my mom hugging me and loving me. I remember playing with my brother shortly after. The truth is my mom never had to tell me I was forgiven; the actions she and my brother did afterward never made me think otherwise. They never threw it in my face. I was never called mean or a thief. I was never called a liar. I was never labeled anything after I made a mistake and repented.

That's what I remember the most. That's what had the most impact on my life. I mean, that's the gospel, right? That's what Jesus does for us. That's the reason I can speak kindly to my daughters and to myself.

As far as I knew, I was still kind. Even after I had done a mean thing to someone very close to me, I was still kind. Yes, it was only fifty cents, but that translates to much larger things in the kingdom, doesn't it? You might be at a point in your life where you've done some really mean things. Maybe you spread a rumor or supported the gossip of another. Maybe you've hurt a friend or loved one. Maybe you've stolen something that doesn't belong to you. Maybe you've done a lot of things. And I want you to know, that's not who you are in Jesus.

The world will label you mean. They will label you a thief. They will label you anything other than what you actually are. To the Messiah, you are a new creation. You are kind. He looks at your mistakes and says, "That is not who you are. Turn away from your sin and back to me."

If you're in this place, I want to give you a few action steps from here because I don't want to leave my beloved readers in this place:

1. Find for yourself someone who loves Jesus and repent to our Father with them. Sometimes, owning up to bigger mistakes is harder to do alone. Know that you have a great defender with you who will uphold you on your path to righteousness. Maybe you don't know anyone;

You Are Because He Is | 13

ask the Lord to bring you to someone, then walk into a church and ask to meet with someone. If you're one of my own, call me. I'll walk with you.

2. Be ready for the earthly consequences. Though we walk in freedom, our sin still has consequences. If you've hurt someone, you might not be given forgiveness as easily as our Father forgives, but I pray you are. When I came to my mom, I was ready to be grounded. I knew what I had done and prepared my heart for it. Ask the Lord to prepare your heart for what's to come, knowing you'll follow our Messiah no matter the earthly consequence.

3. Apologize to whom you need to apologize. Be specific and own the sin you committed against them.

4. Walk in freedom. It's yours because our Messiah freely gave it to you. Goodness, that's loaded, isn't it? What does that even look like? For that, we

look to Paul's word in Galatians. When you live in the freedom of our Messiah, you are given the beautiful gift of the Holy Spirit. You live in the fruit of that gift. Freedom looks like joy, love, peace, kindness, goodness, faithfulness, humility, and self-control. It looks like all of these; it feels like all of these.

Sweet friend, things are sometimes hard. And we don't always make the best decisions. I know. I've been there and will be there again. But these things don't get to define you as mean or cruel. They don't get to put a label on you. But there is one who does label you. He lived a life as a kind man to the fullest because He was the only one who could. Dear friend, you are kind because our Messiah gifted us with the very spirit that makes us kind.

WORTHY

ne night, I was singing to our girls when my oldest began to cry. I stopped and asked her what was going on in her heart. Through the sobs, she began to tell me all about her struggles.

It had been a long day for her. She had to be corrected a lot earlier that day. And there, before bedtime, the weight of her decisions came in the form of shame, a feeling I knew all too well. My heart sank for her. That is not where I want her to live, in the shadow of her mistakes.

I looked at her and my first thought was, "Oh, Lord, how I have failed at showing her Jesus." My second was a prayer, "Lord, give her vision, the vision you have of her."

It was in that prayer that I found holy direction. This was it. This was my opportunity to explain the gospel to her. I may have made mistakes by not showing her the full gospel before but this was my chance to be the hands and feet of Jesus.

There on her bed, I explained the full gospel to her.

By doing that, I told her, her worth. Because our worth is measured by a most holy man, and that man's sinless life, death, and resurrection is who our Father sees when he looks at us. It's who he sees when he looks at our oldest daughter. As I shared this with her, I could see her whole attitude shift to freedom from the shame the gospel delivers. She no longer felt the weight of her mistakes. She was able to separate her day from who she is, and when we can do that, we truly understand our worth.

My favorite example of this biblically is Peter. Jesus looked at Peter wholly in light of the resurrection. Because of His divinity, He saw the man who faithfully followed Him, denied Him, and claimed Him all in a single glance. Peter could have and, by our humanity's measure, should have been discounted in worth. How could he outwardly deny the Messiah and yet be wholly saved by Him? In worldly measure, he isn't. But we aren't talking about that measure. We aren't talking about our standards. We're talking about our God, the author of our worth. By His measure, Peter was forever worthy of the kingdom.

When he denied Jesus out of fear of man, I see myself. When I hear the rooster and see him weep, I see the gospel come to life. His actions did not discount him from His kingdom's worth because his weeping led to repentance. He turned back to the Lord. He gave his life to serve his Messiah and see the kingdom grow. How do we know this? We see him after the resurrection, discipling others through his Messiah.

As I sat on the bed and told this to our daughter, I highlighted to her how our actions don't define us when we choose Jesus.

This doesn't mean we are always free from the earthly consequences of our sins. It does mean that we *never* have to question our worth because of our sins.

Choosing Jesus means we turn back to our Father. When we do that, we have to know that we are not discounted or tossed aside. We have to know that we are immediately redeemed, and shame is no friend of ours. Peter turned back and owned the namesake given by the Messiah. He became a rock for believers and a leader for the church.

We may not have *rock* in our name or even be a leader of the church, but we do have a very unique place in the kingdom that is set aside for us, a place that Jesus brings us to and will continue to forever. It is in this place I find worth and where you can find your worth. Under the wing of my Messiah is where I can see myself clearly. If I know I am worthy, the consequence of my actions becomes a part of my turning back. I don't face them in shame. I face them in repentance, and I do not face them alone.

As Paul tells us in Romans, we are free in our Messiah. Even in our earthly consequences, we are free. When we choose the latter, we can choose to stand on that as we turn back to our Father. We can choose to face the earthly consequences of our sin with freedom, turning back at every moment, and never questioning our worth.

You Are Because He Is | 21

That's what I aim to steward our girls and myself as an adult. We have a Father who doesn't question our worth when we turn back to Him. We may have consequences we must face, but we have a choice on how we face them.

Shame and guilt have no place in a heart that clings tightly to Jesus.

Even in your lowest moments when it feels like you're not worth anything, you have a rescuer who says, "That isn't close to the truth. I will cover you."

And you have a Father who looks at you and simply says, "You are worthy because My son is worthy. Forever."

In the moments when you're feeling less than yourself and when the world is telling you, you aren't worthy of anything, be humble enough to say, "You might think I'm not, but I stand by the Messiah who is. That will forever mean I *am* worthy."

WHOLE

Sometimes things happen to us that leave us feeling broken and unable to see the bigger picture, like having a piece of our heart missing, never to return.

When I was in high school, I got my heart broken. I remember crying on my bed, and my dad coming in to console me. To help me walk through this heartbreak. I can close my eyes and see my tears while crying out to my dad. He probably still can too. He consoled me and let me cry. Let me have my moments of heartbreak. Then once calm and ready, he walked me out of my room while still very much carrying the hurt of a teenage breakup but ready to be presentable.

A few weeks after that, my parents sat me down and asked me if I wanted to go see my aunt in California for a few weeks that summer. Excitedly, I said, "Of course!" Anything to get me out of the place where I could only see my heartbreak.

A few weeks later, I was on a plane. I spent that

time finding joy with my extended family in California, feeling like my hurt was a little bit further away than before. When I came back, my hurt was still there, but I was able to move forward easier and stronger. I now had something tangible to hold onto as I looked ahead, a tangible example of the bigger picture. I saw more of the world, more of what I was growing up into, and more to be ready for. Looking back now, I know what my parents were doing, and if you're a parent, you probably know too. They wanted to give me a taste of the bigger picture, a look at the larger world than just my high school and heartache.

They *wanted* me to tangibly see the bigger picture, the world on the other side of my hurt. It was but a small moment of the larger story of my life. What I don't think they expected was to teach me more about being whole than I had ever known and to teach me more about the kingdom than I had ever expected.

I think of that summer often through every big or

little heartbreak that makes me believe my heart is forever broken, that I am forever broken. The reality is this is the kingdom. The little moments in our lives, the small paragraphs that make up our story are just that, small parts of the story of the coming kingdom. That summer reminds me to keep my eyes on the bigger picture. To keep my eyes on the kingdom because perspective changes the way we see circumstances, and if I can see my circumstance differently, my circumstance no longer has control over me.

When left with no husband and no father-in-law, a brokenhearted Ruth chose to follow her God and His people. She saw the bigger picture of the kingdom despite her pain. She knew the story was not broken because her God was not broken; therefore, she was not broken. Her devout faith proved to be so powerful that her bloodline would birth the Messiah. She never saw that come to fruition on this side of heaven, but she kept her eyes on the kingdom because she knew who held the pieces.

That's what I want you to do with me. I want you to own your wholeness despite your hurt, despite the pieces. It doesn't mean we don't mourn, we don't hurt, but it does mean we don't ever have to believe we are forever broken.

When I was walking through losing our son at twenty-four weeks in the womb, the early days were rough. I couldn't bear to look at myself in the mirror because the whole person I knew before was no longer there. There was a broken woman who I did not know. In one of those raw moments, the Lord sweetly spoke to me the names of other women who had walked through this before me. When I heard their names, brokenness did not come to my mind. Wholeness came to mind. Then the Lord reminded me that when He looked at me, He didn't see a broken person; He saw a whole mended one, put together by the only one who could put me together. Through those women, He delivered to me a perspective, a kingdom view of myself much

You Are Because He Is | 27

farther down the grief road. I was still hurting and still crying all the time. The mirror was still hard. Yet broken was never a word I used to describe myself again even if I felt it.

This is what I want you to know. I want you to know what our Father sees when He looks at you and your hurt and when He looks at you and sees your pain. He doesn't see the broken person you see. He sees the resurrected Messiah who sits at the right hand for you. He sees the fullness of His kingdom in you. He sees the bigger picture of redemption and the kingdom.

You could never be broken in the kingdom where brokenness has no place. You are covered by the one person who makes us whole.

If you're feeling broken, if you've ever felt broken, this is for you. A sweet hug from another who has also looked in the mirror and claimed being broken instead of being whole, a sweet reminder that brokenness is not the gospel, and a reminder that there was another one broken for your hurt and your pain and came out whole, so you could too.

You are whole, dear friend, because the one who broke for us makes us whole again.

GOOD

First and foremost, let's establish the opposite of good, so we know what we're working with. Now, you're probably thinking, "Duh, bad!" but that's not the biblical opposite, is it?

The biblical opposite of good is evil. So if you're not good, then the opposite must be true. I could probably end this chapter right now because no one I know wants to claim evil, yeah?

But it's not always that clear-cut, is it? We don't claim evil, but we also don't claim good simply because most of the time we don't believe we are good. If I took a guess, if you're reading this as a believer, you're thinking something along the lines of, "Well yeah, because I'm a sinner, and by that definition, I'm not good."

But that's not the kingdom. I don't care if you're a sinner. I care that you know that in the kingdom, you are not what you do. Remember those two chapters back?

When one of our daughters was younger, she got

frustrated with her sister and pushed her then immediately started crying. I consoled all the tears and dished out consequences and discipline. Five minutes later, there they were, playing together again, laughing and giggling, like an insane breakdown didn't just happen. You wouldn't have been able to tell who had pushed who because there was freedom.

As an adult, I've made some choices I'm not happy with, little and big. One of those was hurting a friend who was dear to me. I remember apologizing to her, and I remember her sweet heart forgiving me. Yet I struggled to come back. I struggled to believe that I was a good friend, that I was good at all. But it's watching my kids in the above scenario countless times that teach me and remind me what is true: that I am not defined by what I do. I am not evil because I make mistakes. I am not evil because I sin. I am good because Jesus is good. It is He that covers me. I do not ever wear my own works, both good and evil, because I only wear the work on the cross and in the tomb, and the work on the cross and in the tomb was good.

In order to understand just how good you are, we have to understand the work on the cross. I'm going to try to do that here because this chapter is the best one to do it in. There was a man who was prophesied about in the Old Testament. A man who would be fully set apart and fulfill the goodness of God. He would redeem God's people and all nations. Everything about his life was prophesied centuries before he was born. He was born a man, yet one with the Father, and fulfilled the prophecy of the coming Messiah. He lived the life we couldn't. He died, and the world went dark. On the third day, He rose again, forever promising that we would do the same. He became our high priest who covers us as we come before the Father.

His perfect, sinless life covers us; and everything we do is filtered through his life, death, and resurrection. If I don't believe myself to be good, then I don't believe myself to be covered by the one who is good.

I will continue to make my mistakes and keep learning. Though I love the Lord, sin still catches me. But sin will never define me. It can't. And it doesn't define you.

You are good because the one who covers you is good.

WISE

As a child, I struggled with never feeling like I was smart enough. My insecurities in my education ran deep. Though my grades reflected that I was in fact smart, it never felt like I was smart enough, like there should have been more, and I should be doing more.

When I first started saying this to our oldest, I said smart. I would rock her as a baby and say, "You are smart." The more I said that the more it just felt wrong. After a few times of saying that, the Lord would reveal why and would give me the truth to replace it with.

Being smart is all relative to what our world says. It is up to the measurements created by this world, and our world is ever-changing. It's not a biblical trait, and it's not something I wanted our girls to put their identity in. To put our identity in something that changes is what brings us to places of deep questioning and deep spiritual suffering.

So a few months after I started saying this to her, I

replaced "smart" with the truth: You are wise. Wisdom is not dependent upon the things of this world; it is dependent on the one who never changes. The one who gives us wisdom freely.

In 1 Corinthians, Paul speaks of wisdom. He shares with the messianic community that they are what the world would define as foolish but continues that God sees them as wise. He goes on to say it's because of one thing: Jesus, the one who embodies wisdom: "And because of him you are in Christ Jesus, who became to us wisdom from God, righteousness and sanctification and redemption" (1 Corinthians 1:30).

I'm an avid runner; I love it. One time, while pushing my two oldest in the stroller, I had to stop because they were struggling with a toy that was in the stroller. The youngest wanted to borrow a toy the oldest wasn't playing with. Our oldest was struggling with letting her. I stopped and got down to my oldest child's level. Before I share with you what I said, I want to remind you that

You Are Because He Is | 39

we believe our kids to be good, first and foremost. We know sin happens, but we identify them as good.

I got down on her level as I said, "You don't have to share. You do what you believe is best. If you choose not to share, I will redirect your sister to something else. You just let me know what you want to do."

My oldest paused for a bit and replied, "Mom, I want to share with her, but it's so hard because I also don't want to."

I looked at her with a heart so full. This is the struggle we face, isn't it? We want to do good things, but we also don't sometimes. I explained to her how I faced the same struggle, but the fact that she was facing this dilemma meant she was already exhibiting the first steps to wisdom. Wisdom isn't just discerning what is right, but the fulfillment of wisdom is doing what is right. I quickly added, "If you choose to share, I will help you get through it."

Our sweet girl decided to share. I need you to know

over the years I've been on both sides of this. I've helped a sibling be redirected because one had decided not to share. Those situations are hard because I think we innately want our kids to share. But that's not the reality for us adults either, is it? And we believe that wisdom and goodness aren't realized by our kids in these moments, practiced? Yes. But it's realized in the everyday moments where big decisions aren't made. It's realized in hearing the gospel over and over.

It's in everyday moments that they realize that they are in fact wise. I can't remind my child she is wise when making tough decisions if she has no basis for that in her everyday life. How do we teach them then? How do we build that foundation for them?

Well, we tell them every day. We read the words with them. One of the very first verses we memorized with our kids was Proverbs 2:6: "For the Lord gives wisdom, from His mouth comes wisdom and understanding."

If we do not know that wisdom is where knowledge

and understanding meet, we do not know what wisdom is. If we do not cling to our father, we are missing a part of ourselves he longs to give us.

We show wisdom to them. We are open to decisions we have to make and are open about how we get to our conclusions. Then perhaps one of the biggest things we can do is to continue to show them we trust who they are. We trust their ability to make a wise choice. There are times we have to step in as parents, but most of the time, we have the ability to walk them very closely through their decisions and consequences. Walking with them through their consequences, both good and bad, gives us the precious moments of pointing them closer to our Messiah.

But maybe your crisis is not that of your kids. Maybe you've made some really awful choices that were not very wise. Quite possibly, you're sitting there, thinking that you aren't wise. The choices you've made do not exhibit wisdom; therefore, you couldn't possibly be wise.

Hi! Nice to meet you. I've been there. I used to live there often. But we've already well established that we are not what we do, yeah?

Our Father in heaven is the keeper and creator of wisdom. His son became wise. His spirit lives in us and delivers us wisdom in every moment, even if we don't always choose it.

I feel the Lord calling this chapter to end in a prayer so let's do that:

Oh Lord, I've made some choices that don't exhibit Your wisdom. It's been difficult to claim wisdom as part of who I am in you lately. Father, forgive me for forgetting that it is a part of me now. Open my eyes to the gift of wisdom that came through the empty tomb through the realization of my identity in the Messiah. Lord, may I remember that I am wise because of the Messiah who made a way for Your spirit to always live in me. Amen.

You Are Because He Is | 43

BEAUTIFUL

When I was in eighth grade, I decided to get a haircut, a major one. Now before I tell you what exactly I decided on, I need to set the stage for you. My face is naturally round, and I rocked a full set of braces from sixth grade until tenth grade. Now after having hair that complimented my facial structure, I decided it would be best to cut it all off to my ears and get straight bangs. Some of you reading this probably remember this haircut and time in my life. And you've given me grace. Bless you.

I look back on pictures from then and think, "What in the world was I thinking?" Do any of you have those fashion moments in your life? I'm sure we all do or will at some point.

The point of me sharing this with you actually has nothing to do with what I thought of myself other than, at the time, I thought I was *beautiful*. And it has everything to do with what my mom taught me during this time. I can remember seeing this for the first time after our hairdresser cut it all off. I digress. I can remember my mom looking at it, then looking me right in the eyes and saying, "You're beautiful." To this day, I know she wasn't lying. I know when she looks at me when she's always looked at me, she sees beauty even during my worst mistakes, simply because she's always seen the light of Messiah in me and has always spoken to that.

My mom really was a trailblazer when it came to empowering women to be who they are. Never on a large scale but always in her home and her circle. And that's where it should be done first, shouldn't it?

It was during small moments like this paired with hearing the word of God that truly gave me a strong foundation about what beauty is and why it is who I am.

There have been moments in my life when I have felt so ugly. Most of those moments have never been about my physical appearance and almost always have been a heart issue that has manifested in me really hating how I looked. Some of those times have been from really awful decisions I made that caused me to feel ugly inside, and that's the worst for me. Sometimes, I just really did not like my physical appearance. Throughout my life, it's been a little bit of everything. Despite what has caused me to believe I am not beautiful, there has been an echo in my heart that I've heard over and over since I was a child: "You are beautiful."

For me, it's my own mother's voice, but really, it's bigger and deeper than that. While my mom set the stage, my Father gave me the identity. It's the voice of my Father in heaven. The voice echoes in the deepest parts of our hearts and says, "I created you in my image," "You are fearfully and wonderfully made," "I knit you in your mother's womb," and "You are a dwelling place for my spirit."

Have you ever read the details of the temple in the Old Testament and the details of how the temple looked? If not, go back and read 1 Kings 7 and 2 Chronicles 4.

What you'll find is this extravagant place that is only fit for the best, fit for our Father to dwell. You'll find colors, gold, and intricate details. While the temple is ultimately a type and shadow of our Messiah and the temple in heaven, it shows just how much God cares about where He dwells and where He rests.

And a part of Him rests in us. His Holy Spirit dwells in us. How much more beautiful are each of us than the most extravagant place here on earth?

There are things like our choice of haircut or our life decisions that will try to tell us something very different from our Father. They will say that we are only as deep as our hair. We are only as deep as our mistakes. We are only as deep as our gym visits. The list goes on. Oh, but, friends, we are much deeper than that. That's easy to say though, isn't it? It's a bit harder to live out.

When I think about what I want for my daughters, it's the same thing I want for all women struggling to hold fast to the beauty inside them—the ability to shift

You Are Because He Is | 49

their perspective from their own to the one who holds the judgment.

Sometimes truth is veiled by perspective. A different one is desperately needed, so we no longer see through the veil of our emotions, assumptions, mistakes, pain, etc. I think of this often when I read the gospels. So many of God's people wore a veil with one perspective, their own. But we aren't called to see things from our own perspective. We're called to see things from the kingdom's perspective. This includes the way we see ourselves. This perspective is one that includes the death and resurrection of Jesus and the one that includes eternity and a never-changing Father. But how do we do this in the trenches? How do we step back and do this practically every day?

Instead of offering you something new, I'd like to remind you of scripture. All too often, we look for a five-step plan for something when our Father has already given us the strategies we need in His word: "You shall bind them as a sign on your hand, they shall be as frontlets between your eyes. You shall talk of them when you sit in your house, when you walk by the way when you lie down, and when you rise up" (Deuteronomy 6).

Whatever you have to do to have God's word saturate your life, you do it. We repeat the same prayer each morning with our kids, which is just scripture. I sing verses to them and me often. A Bible is left open on our table all the time. Anything I can do to have my eyes constantly shifted to where my perspective should live, I will. Here is a prayer for you paired with a few verses for you to write somewhere and sing to yourself, so you can immediately repeat it in the moments you don't feel so beautiful:

> Lord, forgive me for not seeing myself as
> You see me. You created me in your image.
> You made me a dwelling place for Your
> perfect and Holy Spirit. You know every
> hair on my head, every freckle on my face,

You Are Because He Is | 51

every wrinkle here and to come. You know every insecurity I have about my body, my weight. May you come in and remind me how wholly beautiful I am because of You. May I fiercely own the fact that I am beautiful. May the definition of my beauty be within your measurement and not of others or things of this world. Amen.

So God created man in his own image, the image of God he created him; male and female. (Genesis 1:27)

Or do you not know that your body is a temple of the Holy Spirit within you, whom you have from God? You are not your own. (1 Corinthians 6:19)

But even the hairs on your head are all numbered. (Matthew 10: 30)

There will be heavy moments and circumstances that will try to define your beauty. But, dear friend, you are not defined by the things of this world. You are defined by the one who knit you together in the womb.

You are beautiful because you were created in the image of the most beautiful one.

WANTED

One of the deepest desires of our hearts is to be wanted. We long to be wanted by our family, spouses, our peers, our colleagues, and our world. It's an innate desire we all have, this sense of belonging. But it gets more complicated than that, doesn't it? It does because we don't just want to be wanted by any family, peer, or colleagues. We want to be wanted by those we feel are important in our lives. We long to be wanted by those we elevate in our own lives. In a lot of ways, this directly ties to our worth.

"I am worthy enough because they want me." Does this sound familiar? It does to me, and it hits parts of my heart that need our Messiah that much more.

When I first started saying this to the girls each day, telling them they were wanted was non-negotiable. I knew I wanted a deep relationship with each of them, and at the core, I wanted them to know that I wanted them and that they would always be wanted. More than that, I longed for them to know they were wanted by the only one who could fulfill the desire to be wanted in us. I knew I could never fulfill that desire. I also knew that as a mom, I could show the love of our Father to them by wanting them to follow the example our Father wants us.

As a military family, we've moved a lot. In ten years of marriage, we have moved eight times. Eight times we've uprooted from our community, packed up our stuff, and filled a different house. With each move, the familiar feeling of, "Will they want me there?" creeps into my heart. "They" being the community where we're headed. My husband's work community, our neighborhood, a church community, other women, and the list goes on. It's a constant feeling I have that likes to creep up with each move we make. While this tangible movement brings the desire to be wanted in my face every time, it doesn't always take a move. Sometimes all it takes to remind me that I have that deep desire is to put something creative out in the world, to long to be successful in my job, ministry, parenting, or any role I take on in this life.

You Are Because He Is | 57

The reality is that where I find the desire to produce good things, I find the desire to be wanted. If we're honest with ourselves, we tie what we do with who we are. That leads to tying our identity with what we do. A frequent lie we love to whisper to ourselves indirectly is, "I am what I do, and if people want what I do, they want me."

In the early moves of our marriage, I used to list all the things I could do once we arrived, all the things I needed to jump into immediately. All these so that I could begin to produce things in our new community and be wanted by others. It didn't take but a few moves and a lot of maturing in Jesus to realize how misplaced my identity was.

To unwind this lie and get to the bottom of what is actually true, I want to turn to one man in the Bible I don't think anyone would want in their circle of friends. I want to look at Judas, the one who betrayed Jesus. The one whom Jesus kept close to Him because He wanted

Judas. Regardless of what Judas was going to do, Jesus wanted him.

Jesus, the one who knew of the betrayal, the one with perfect vision and perfect character of God, wanted the man who would ultimately send Him to the cross. I don't want to get into what I would do or want because that isn't what defines me. What defines me is the one who wanted Judas. Therefore, my sole focus is on why Jesus would want this man in His closest circle. The answer is simple really: We serve a good God who wants us always. When the world thinks we're hopeless or we don't belong, we serve a savior who says the opposite. He says, "You are not hopeless, and you will always belong."

If we want to deeply know who we are, we have to deeply know the character of the one who created us. If we want to know the character of the one who deeply created us, we read the word He left us. If we read His word, we will constantly see a God who always wants His children and a God who constantly gives and gives

You Are Because He Is | 59

so that His creation can grow closer to Him because He wants His creation. He has always wanted us close and near Him because He has loved us from the beginning.

His character does not change. The fact that He wants His children will never change; therefore, you, my friend, will *always* be wanted.

The desire to be wanted is not a bad thing. We were created to be wanted by the one who created us. However, we severely misplaced that desire a lot. The desire does not belong in each move our family makes, it does not belong in my community, and it doesn't even belong in my family. First and foremost, it belongs in the hands of Jesus. It will always belong there because it is where you will always genuinely and lovingly be wanted.

Let's say an honest prayer together:

Father, I long to be wanted. I long to be wanted by those around me. Forgive me for misplacing this desire outside of you. You have always and will always want me. You don't look at what I do and want me based on those things. You simply want me because you are love. You want me because you are good. You want me because you created me to be wanted by you. May I always remember that I am wanted deeply by you, and may I know that you wanting me is always more than enough.

You are wanted, sweet friend, because the one who sees the whole picture always wants you. Always.

GENTLE

I come from a large extended family. I'm one of the younger ones in my generation of cousins, and there are a lot of us. Growing up, we'd always have a huge Christmas Eve party where we all got together at someone's house, and joy was shared around a meal—let's be honest—around tamales. I can close my eyes and see all my aunts and uncles laughing. I can see my older cousins chatting away and catching up. I can see the younger ones running around the house. I can see it all. But more than seeing it, I can hear it, and above everything, I hear the women, all the women swapping stories of their kids, recipes, the year, and all the laughter and joy. Maybe it's because I knew, one day, that would be me, I would be one of the women in the group, so I focused on their voices, the voices of my future. I knew that one generation behind them was me. So I listened to them, I focused on them, and I wanted to soak it all in.

I can hear them laughing in the kitchen, egging on their husbands, correcting their kids. I hear it all.

And they were loud. The whole house was loud, but the women, I could hear them over everything. Their voice could stop me dead in my tracks even today. The loud voice was telling me to slow down as she carried a plate of food. The voices asked me about my schooling and sports.

I knew to listen and honor their words. They were firm and direct when it came to discipline and direction. And yet, the same women who could steal a room with their personality, hugged so gently as they would say, "Aye, Mijita, you're so beautiful." I can still remember my aunt being so gentle with me that summer I spent with her. After my heart felt so broken, she was what I needed. The firm, fun, steal-a-room, and gentle-spirit woman gave me a taste of our Father again.

It's the faces of the women in my family, my mom, my aunts, my cousins, that I saw when I began to say, "You are gentle," to our oldest daughter. They are all so different but all so gentle. I'm not sure the world would classify them as gentle, but I'm not here to measure with those standards. I measure with that of the kingdom. I knew deeply that our girls could be whoever they were *and* be gentle. I knew this first and foremost because of the examples I had growing up. I would be an adult before I understood exactly what the Holy Spirit does for us.

It was as an adult when I understood what a relationship with my Messiah looked like that I understood gentleness doesn't belong to any type of person. Gentleness doesn't fight against the extrovert. It doesn't belong to the quiet; it belongs to you, and it belongs to me.

It belongs to the one whom the spirit dwells in. I used to believe that I had to be quieter and toned down in my personality to be gentle. That's not the kingdom. That's not the kingdom at all.

Ruth, gentle Ruth, if you haven't guessed, she's a favorite of mine in the Bible. I can't wait to meet her. Anyway, our dear Ruth is being told over and over by

Naomi to not come back to Judah. It's not until she has pushed back enough to let Naomi know that she is not budging; she's not going back to Moab. Now I'm not sure the ins and outs of Ruth's personality, but here's what I do know: she was brave, bold, *and* gentle with her mother-in-law. The easier choice would have been to return to her people where she could easily remarry. However, Ruth followed her God, and in turn, all the things wrapped up into one. She was brave as she traveled to a land she did not know with a family she was not born into. She was bold to speak to her mother-in-law the way she did, and she was gentle enough that Naomi's heart was soft toward her after she was so bold. They were not separate; they were all there.

That's the kingdom. That's the reality of who we are. I'll say it again: it doesn't just belong to any one type of person; it belongs to the ones in whom the spirit dwells. It's one of the sweetest gifts the Holy Spirit gives us. It is who we are when we are made new. It is a part of us.

It belongs to the person whose voice could carry in a crowded restaurant to say, "Oh, hey! It's me!" It belongs to the person who doesn't enjoy large gatherings. It belongs to the person who leads fiercely. It belongs to the person who follows well. Simply because when Jesus made a way for us to be restored to what we were always supposed to be, he gave us the very spirit that breeds gentleness.

Sister, don't let the enemy tell you that you're too much to be gentle. Don't let the enemy tell you that you're too quiet to be gentle. Fill in the blank with any "You're too _____ to be gentle." It's not true. It never will be true to the Messiah.

Sweet friend, you are gentle because the Messiah made a way for you to always be gentle.

NEEDED

I am a military spouse. I have seen my husband through a deployment, more field exercises than I can count, and even more TDYs. For all my civilian friends, a TDY is when the soldier leaves temporarily for another assignment, anywhere from a week to five months. Didn't know you'd be getting some army acronyms in here, did you?

I say this to say that I have seen more transitions of my husband leaving for a short bit than I'd ever like to see. These transitions are always rough for everyone. The house feels like it's falling apart for a good week before it starts to feel like things are kind of OK. The girls and I are trying to figure out how to fill the hole Dad fits perfectly in and that's difficult.

How does bedtime without Dad look? I know for a fact when he's here, there is not this much crying or asking for water. Wait, when does trash come again? He took it out for us. How do we do our nightly Bible reading without our main guy? We pivot and adjust. We

70 | *Annalisa Barraza*

pivot and adjust for every moment, but it still doesn't ever feel like it's how it should be.

That's because Dad is needed in our home. There is a spot that he fits perfectly into. We say the same for every person in our family. Each is needed, and we each fit the hole that was created for us in our little family.

That's how the body of the Messiah works. A small image of what it means to be a part of this body in the kingdom. Paul writes to the church of Corinth on this very topic. He first tells them that they are one body, he's talking about unity here. He goes on to compare the body of the Messiah to a literal human body. So we're unified, but we're also diverse. The eye cannot be the arm, and the foot cannot be the ear. If you're not catching on, let me put it to you very plainly. Someone else cannot do what you were created to do. Period.

You were handcrafted uniquely and wonderfully. Your diversity and who you are matter. Are you unified

You Are Because He Is | 71

in the body? Yes! Were you created for something only you could do? Yes!

Do we figure out how to function successfully when Dad leaves for a bit? Yes! Is it wonky and difficult? Yes!

Make no mistake, God will use the body to get things done, but it might take a little more stretching of members as He brings the body together to do so. I also don't want to give the impression of just the big things, like the calling on your life or the big things you will do. I am talking about the tiny, everyday moments you do each day—the people you speak to at work, the kids you're raising, and the wave you give to the same person each day. Those are the moments you need. The big ones too, but do not mistake the little ones as less important.

We like to look at the bigger calling God has on our life to apply this kingdom truth. We think that we are only needed for that larger calling. The reality is that we are needed for the small moments just as much, if not more, because those moments happen within the framework of the larger one. I think back to Ruth again. She was needed in the greater kingdom picture of Jesus. But in her everyday life, Ruth was needed for the children of God. She needed to help Naomi see her God again and to be in the life of Boaz. She caused a turning back toward God for those closest to her, and that matters. Don't downplay how much you are needed in your everyday life, in the everyday moments of school, work, errands, family, all of it.

If you ever find yourself believing that you are no longer needed, let me offer you this. While we figure things out around the house when Dad is gone and get in our own little rhythm, we welcome him back joyfully. We do it because things become immensely easier again. The weight of carrying something that is not ours to carry is taken off, and we welcome him back with open arms.

So let's squash that lie. You are always needed. The body of the Messiah will feel lighter as you step back to who you were created to be.

LOVED BY GOD

Honestly, I could leave this chapter alone at the title and be done. If you know God and now walk with Him, you know this. This is driven home so much in the church, as it should be. However, a large number of Christians still struggle with shame at one point in their life or question the love God has for them when sorrow or struggle hits. So maybe there is more to this.

I've struggled with shame, the shame of thinking God looks at me as less than. So we say this to the girls too, "You are loved by God, and there is nothing that you could ever do that would change that truth." This is an absolute, friend. He loves us in a holy way. The best way. Even if we don't believe in Him at times. Even when sorrow, rejection, or struggle hits, He loves you. He's the only one who can love you like this.

In case the rest of the chapters didn't drive the good news home, let me take the opportunity to do that now. God created man in His image. He formed you, knew your name, and has held a special place for you ever since. When man fell into temptation, the love God had for His children didn't waver. In fact, it was at that point the plan for redemption and sacrifice He was ready to give began to unfold, all to culminate in the life, death, and resurrection of His son and our Messiah, Jesus. I know this has been told over and over again, but this is a weighty matter that needs to captivate our hearts so that we no longer fall into the shame or rejection of this world again.

I'm a mom to four little girls. We homeschool and spend our days together. On any given day, there is a list a mile long of things I've done wrong by 10:00 a.m. I lose my temper, I pick up my phone instead of playing, I dismiss things, and the list goes on. It's easy for me to take into account all these things at the end of my day. I can sit and dwell on them until I'm up at midnight, making a list of how I am going to be better the next day, trying to fight my shame with another list. But that's not the kingdom.

You Are Because He Is | 77

God looks at the list, and where we see our shortcomings, He sees a different list. He sees the merit of Jesus and the pure righteousness of His son. He sees that in us and says, "I am so pleased with her!" So instead, His list looks like this: She hugged her daughter while she cried over spilled juice, she helped her daughter tie her shoes, and she said prayers before the day even began. A list that I don't ever run through.

I want to be clear that we are not what we do, and God's love for us is not determined by the list He creates. However, the way we tend to see only our failings, the Lord sees all our strengths all the time because He fiercely loves us. That will never change. Jesus sealed that in His resurrection. When shame tries to inch its way into your heart, I hope that you also see all that the Lord sees, all that He is pleased within you because He is so pleased with your righteousness.

The love of God is not based on circumstance; it's based on who He is. And He is never changing forever.

He is a promise keeper, which means His love is infinite, which means you cannot run out of it, and it does not waver.

When I was pregnant with our fourth baby, I was gifted this beautiful little frame. On the frame were the words, "You are so loved."

I looked at that frame again while writing this chapter and was instantly taken back to meeting each of our girls. There was an immense amount of emotion, so much emotion. In me, there was joy, fear, and excitement bubbling up. But the feeling I felt toward our daughters was different than any other emotion I've ever felt. There weren't butterflies and glitter swirling around in my vision, creating a warmth in me. It was a renewed strength and boldness in my heart that wanted to explode. It wanted to be loud, and I knew that this emotion would do whatever in its power to love and protect these babies.

It's that emotion that I thought of as I reread those framed words, and I giggled a bit. It's not what you

You Are Because He Is | 79

picture, is it? The love for a child? The truth is the love I feel for our girls doesn't always feel the same. Sometimes it feels like butterflies. Sometimes it feels like a deep sadness when they experience hurt. Sometimes it feels like a fierce need to protect. It's all so different, which is why the love of God cannot be defined by how we feel.

The love of God tends to get the reputation of the warm butterflies with a soft filter applied to the lens. However, that is the example our human hearts have projected onto our God. The reality is that the love of God cannot be tied down to an earthly feeling because it was never meant to be. Instead, He gave us His word—stories and books that complete the biggest story that tells us who He is—to remind us that He is a God of the covenant, and He has held us from the womb. He knows us and created us in His image.

He places His love within the definition of absolute, Him. In order to drive it home, He faithfully sent the

Messiah, His son, to fulfill the love He has for us. The love He has had for us since creation.

His fulfillment on the cross of every single word spoken to His people is what He has given us to define His love. This means when you begin to doubt His love for you, you can undoubtedly call that lie out. When our thoughts and emotions want to tell us that God cannot possibly love us, we can stand on the pure truth that the love of God is not based on what we think or how we feel.

His love endures. It is steadfast. And it is yours.

> The steadfast love of the Lord never ceases; his mercies never come to end.
> (Lamentations 3:22)

LOVED BY MOM AND DAD

"**Y**ou are loved by Mom and Dad. And there is nothing you could do that could ever change that," I whisper last. Usually, at this time, the girls are nuzzling their heads up against mine, letting me know that they hear me. Saying this is one of my favorite parts to tell them simply because I know what my love for them is based on making this statement insanely true in my heart.

Let me pause for a second and honor those for this may not be true for those who have walked and lived with the very deep hurt of a mother or father's lack of love in their life. I pray the chapter preceding this one spoke to the depths of your heart, to the very depths and places where the lack of a parent's love touched. I pray that if you have kids of your own, this chapter speaks to you in ways that bring your parenting heart to life.

My heart is for you because our Father's heart is for you. He steps in with a much deeper love than an earthly mother and father ever could. My hope is that you never waver in the love that is given to you and the love that covers you.

It is from that love, the love of God, that my love for our girls is based. As parents, one of the greatest gifts that we get to steward is the ability to give our kids a taste of the Father's love. Before they come to know Him intimately, they'll know you. However, it is up to us how we steward such a gift.

The stewardship of this gift is not based on circumstance or our own emotions. Much like what I've covered in the pages of this book, the theme that our identity and love cannot be based on anything other than that of our Messiah is the heart of this chapter. If we choose to base our love on anything else, exceptions begin to slip in.

There was a time in my early twenties when my mom and I just didn't get along. I had grown into a pretty rebellious time when it came to a relationship with God,

You Are Because He Is | 85

and it reflected in my relationship with my own mom. I fought her. I fought every little thing she said. It made it impossible to have a good, solid relationship with her. To every credit to my mom, she stuck that time out. She kept coming to see me. She kept showing up. She kept calling.

I can look back at that season and see it for what it really was. I was rebelling against God and His hand in my life. However, because my parents had done such an incredible job showing me unconditional love, my rebellion manifested toward them, specifically toward my mom simply because she had been one of the greatest tangible examples of unconditional love to me.

Make that make sense! Why would I want to rebel against the person who loved me the most? I get that answer from His word. Over and over again, we see the children of God rebel against God, the God who loves them unconditionally. It was the state of my heart. And the state of my heart needed to intimately meet the one who saves.

***

The perseverance of my own mother in my life was the example I needed when I decided to stop running from a relationship with Jesus. She showed me, as best as an earthly mother could, that there was a love that was so deep and real, that it could overrule the things I've done. It was because of her example during my hardest years that I had a better picture of how God loves me.

After walking that out, I knew the kind of mother I wanted to be. I wanted to be the mother who loved like Jesus. I wanted to be the mother who loved them so deeply that it pointed them back to the one who loves me and who loves them. I knew that even on my best days, I'd fail in some sort of way. But more than knowing that, I trusted that on my best and worst days, Jesus would shine through and fill in all those spots I miss.

Loving our kids unconditionally seems like a

no-brainer because our love for them was never based on what they did, right? We automatically think of all the things children can do wrong in our eyes and say, "Of course, I'd still love them!"

However, I want to push this narrative a bit. I want to push it because loving our kids unconditionally also means that we willingly die for ourselves every single day and show them how to do the same. Loving our kids unconditionally means that we are willing to live and let the Holy Spirit do work in us here and now, in those moments where you want to give into your own apathy or laziness or escape via the scroll. You know the ones I'm talking about. Those moments have the ability to show our kids just how much we love them unconditionally. It's in those moments when we get to demonstrate our unconditional love to our children. They demonstrate to our children that the love given to us is bigger than the things of this world. It demonstrates hope beyond our own deeds and beyond our own hands. Those moments sanctify our parenting flesh. They let our children see that there is something much bigger than our own emotions, our apathy, our lack of motivation, and our desire to escape by scrolling through social media. And His name is Jesus.

Of course, I'd love our children no matter what they did, but do I love them enough to train them in righteousness right now? Do I love them enough to give my example of picking up my own cross and following Jesus? To show them the never-ending well where my unconditional love for them flows from?

Our girls are still young, and in this season, loving them unconditionally looks a lot like being late because there was a teachable moment we didn't pass up. It looks like flour and eggs all over the counter because they're learning to bake. It looks like putting my phone down for most of the day as I disciple little people. It looks like waking up early to get my heart focused on the Lord

You Are Because He Is | 89

before they wake up. It looks like taking the time to teach them the same thing over and over until it hits.

For me in my rebellious twenties, unconditional love looked like my mom showing up. It looked like her constantly just being there for me, letting me know she was still around and still loved me, and filling in my needs in very real tangible ways. Unconditional love as a parent of littles also looks a lot like showing up, doesn't it?

We get that example from the one who constantly shows up for us in different ways at different points of our lives but show up He does. He shows up when we're able to stop scrolling and be present. He shows up when we feel like we're at the end of our parenting rope. He shows up on our best days and during our worst days. That is my example to follow.

May we give an example of the love of God to our children in such a way that introduces them to their sweet and loving Messiah.

UNCHANGING

Growing up, I had this view of a distant God. I carried a lot of shame for one reason or another, and it caused me to view God as someone who saw me that same way. I always knew God loved me, but being told that He loved me couldn't win out on the perception I had of Him.

What I came to find out was I was viewing God through a veil of brokenness, but God was never looking at me like that. It wasn't one moment that brought me to Him, but there was one particular moment that I remember things starting to shift.

I had just had our first daughter. I was being flaky and unreliable with my dearest friend at the time. One night, I had pushed the limits of our friendship, and it was time to call me out. This wasn't new to me. I had never been able to be a good friend to people before this moment. When I got overwhelmed or felt too stretched, I'd become flaky and avoid hard conversations instead of just addressing the fact that I was overwhelmed or depressed. More on that in a bit.

She called me, and I answered, ready for the accusation that I wouldn't be able to defend, ready to grieve this friendship too. But when I picked up the phone and heard her voice, it wasn't anger, it wasn't even hurt. It was compassion. I'll never forget her voice on the other end of the line saying, "This isn't who you are." She continued by telling me that whatever was going on, she was there for me. In her eyes, it didn't matter how flaky I had been, how terrible a friend I had been. She was going to be there for me. Shortly after that conversation and a few others, I sought help for postpartum depression from my doctor, and I started talking to Jesus again.

I share this with you because what she said to me was the first time I really heard that what I was doing wasn't who I was. I started to view God differently. It would take years more for me to really come home to the fact that God wasn't the one who changed. I was.

Before I started talking to Jesus again, I just assumed that God saw only the broken parts and that there was

You Are Because He Is | 93

no possible way that God would see me as anything else. I had this distorted image that I needed to get better, to do better, so God would see me as worthy. But the gospel isn't based on our works, is it, friends?

It's based on Jesus.

My dear friend turned best friend showed me early on how God views His creation. He's looking at us through the lens of His son's death and resurrection. He was looking at you through that lens when the decisions you made hurt others. He was looking at you through that lens when the decisions of others hurt you. He was looking at you through that lens when you chose Him. And He's looking at you through that lens now.

One night after I was done telling our girls that there was never anything they could do to change ours or God's love for them, they started running down a list of scenarios then ending it with, "Would you still love me then?"

You can only imagine how that rabbit hole went. Eventually, I stopped them, and I said this,

"Your decisions will bring different consequences. We will even need to discipline you sometimes, and to you, it may feel like we don't love you at times, but I can assure you, our love for you will never change."

I said that because that has been true to what I know about God. I know my actions have real consequences, both positive and negative. I know that I am disciplined out of love to bring me out of sin. And I know that there have been times when I have felt unloved in my life. But what I feel and what is true do not always align.

I know how God sees me, how He loves me because He told me. He has repeatedly written in His word how He feels about His people. How He rescues them because He loves them. How He shows up for them because He loves them. How He disciplines them because He loves them. How He went to war and won against the enemy because He loves them. Because He loves us.

So when I talk about an unchanging love, I am speaking about a God who never changed, who has never

You Are Because He Is | 95

wavered in His character, and who has always viewed us through His son, Jesus.

It was never Him who was changing. It was us.

I want to end with a prayer for you, friend. As I close this book, I want to bless you.

May you know that you are brave, kind, worthy, whole, good, wise, beautiful, wanted, gentle, needed, and loved by God. Amen.

ACKNOWLEDGMENTS

Mom and Dad, thank you for being the first to believe in this before I even did. This was written based on the foundation you set for me and from the dreams you saw in me long before I did. I could never thank you enough for all that you do for me even now.

Team Vivo, thank you for encouraging me unlike any other. Outside of my family, you've gone to bat for me over and over. This book was breathed partially from the way you've spoken into my life and over life.

Joey, Julianna, Leia, Hosanna, and Eliza, thank you for loving me and encouraging me to take this step of faith and making room for this to happen. This is for you, written on the fringes of our beautiful life and created from the life the Lord gave us. You're forever my people, inspiring me to be better than the day before. I love you more.